AMERICAN EVENTS

BY
Henry Freeman

Table of Contents

AD 1863- Emancipation Proclamation issued
AD 1865- Lincoln assassinated and Reconstruction begins

The Nation Grows
AD 1869- First Transcontinental Railroad completed
AD 1870- Gilded Age begins
AD 1870- Standard Oil Co. created
AD 1875- Carnegie opens first steel mill
AD 1876- Telephone invented
AD 1892- Homestead Strike
AD 1898- Spanish American War
AD 1908- Ford Model T first sold
AD 1917- American enters World War I
AD 1920- Roaring Twenties begin
AD 1929- Stock Market Crash and beginning of Great Depression
AD 1933- New Deal begins

America as a World Leader
AD 1941- Japanese attack on Pearl Harbor
AD 1945- America uses first atomic weapons
AD 1947- Truman Doctrine and Marshall Plan outline foreign policy
AD 1955- Rosa Parks and the bus boycott
AD 1968- Martin Luther King, Jr. assassinated
AD 1969- Moon landing
AD 1975- Vietnam War ends
AD 1981- Reagan becomes president
AD 1991- First Gulf War in Iraq
AD 2001- 9/11 Terrorist Attacks
AD 2007- The Great Recession begins
AD 2008- Barack Obama elected president

Pre-Columbian Era

13,500 BCE- Migration of hunter-gatherers from Beringia

The history of the Unites States of America began thousands of years before the idea of "America" even existed. During the last Ice Age, circa 13,500 BCE, a group of hunter-gatherers came to North America. These people, known as Paleo-Indians, crossed into what is today modern Alaska from Russia via a land bridge called Beringia located in the modern Bering Strait. Scholars theorize that these people were merely following the wild game, which was their primary food source. As the Paleo-Indians moved south, they found land that was significantly easier to inhabit and began spreading out, owing to an ever-increasing food supply. Over the next several millennia, many more groups of Paleo-Indians crossed the land bridge, until plate tectonics caused the bridge to submerge. After that, no new settlers would come to North America for millennia. The populations of these people began to increase greatly, and over time, these groups spread as far south as the southern tip of South America. Hundreds of distinct cultures emerged and developed until Europeans finally began to explore the Americas.

AD 1000- Viking exploration of the New World

During the millennia between the divergence of European/Asian populations and the populations of the New World, Europe developed many warlike, feudal cultures. As land ownership was the basis of these cultures, there was a need for ever more territory. This led to all corners of Europe being explored and populated. In an effort to settle new land, a group of Europeans known as Vikings settled several islands to the west of mainland Europe. In an effort to discourage other groups from similar exploration, one of their greatest chiefs, Erik the Red, named his home island Iceland. This name was a severe misnomer, as the island was warm and easy to farm. To keep other tribes from his land, Erik named a large island to the west Greenland. The irony is that all but the smallest portion of Greenland was covered in ice and uninhabitable. Seeking a domain of his own, Erik's son, Leif, set out across the Atlantic Ocean with a party in longboats, making landfall in modern Newfoundland. Although the area was rich in fish, the soil was not particularly rich, meaning that Viking settlement in the New World was never permanent, and within one hundred years, all of the settlements had been abandoned.

AD 1492- Columbus'   famous first journey

The 1300's and 1400's in Europe were a time of expansion and explosion of technology. Sailors found new sea-routes to India and China, although the routes were fraught with danger. In an effort to find an expedited way to India, a young Italian named Christopher Columbus convinced the Spanish crown to finance an expedition west. Columbus believed that the Orient could be reached in this way, and, in accordance with the predominate geographical arithmetic of the time, believed that the world was too small to hold a landmass west of Europe but east of Asia. Columbus left Europe with three ships, the *Nina, Pinta,* and *Santa Maria*. On October 12, 1492, the Columbian voyage reached an island that Columbus named San Salvador. Due to the errors in his arithmetic, he falsely believed that he had reached India, and therefore named the natives he encountered "Indians." On October 28th of that year, Columbus reached, and began exploring, the modern island of Cuba. Columbus returned to Spain as a hero and prepared for another voyage to the New World, this time with settlement in mind. Although Columbus never found a direct water-route westward to India, his exploits spurred further exploration of North America and eventually led to its settlement by Europeans.

Early English Settlements

AD 1607- Jamestown is founded

While Spanish explorers tended toward exploration for resource exploitation, English explorers favored settlement. In 1607, an exploration funded by the London Company reached the eastern shores of modern-day Virginia. To honor the King of England, who had granted permission for the voyage, the exploration named the settlement Jamestown. This was the first permanent English settlement in the New World. Other explorations had set up colonies (most infamously, the "Lost Colony" of Roanoke), but all had failed for various reasons. Life in Jamestown was difficult, and during the first year, many settlers died due to illness or starvation. The Jamestown colony would not have survived without the help of the Powhatan Indians who were native to the region. At first, native-colonist relations were cordial, but over time, it became clear that the settlers had expansion in mind, at which point relations began to deteriorate. Over the winter of 1609-1610, the colony underwent a massive famine known as the "Starving Time" during which as many as eighty percent of the colonists died. Jamestown was also famous for another "first"; the first African slave in America was brought to Jamestown. Amid these events, Jamestown began a tradition of self-governance that would become the cornerstone of the American political system.

AD 1620- Founding of Plymouth Colony

Another foundational principal of the America was religious toleration. In the mid-1610's, a group of religious dissenters in England known as the Separatists (or more commonly, the Pilgrims) left England in search of a place where they could worship freely. After time in Holland, the group petitioned the King of England for the right to settle in the New World. A group of these settlers arrived off the coast of Massachusetts in the ship *Mayflower*. Prior to disembarking, the Pilgrims signed the Mayflower Compact, which is considered the first document of self-government created by the English in the New World. On December 21, 1620, Pilgrims stepped ashore at Plymouth and began the process of establishing housing. Although the colony survived its first winter, it was hard-pressed to feed its members, and without the help of the local natives, the colony would likely have failed. In response to the natives helping with the colony's first harvest in 1621, the two groups set aside a time of "thanksgiving" to celebrate their joint success.

AD 1639- The Fundamental Orders of Connecticut is signed

From the 1620's well into the 1640's, the colonies in America underwent rapid expansion, both in size and number. Inevitably, disagreements over governance and culture took place between the colonists. For those whose views were dismissed, settling elsewhere seemed an ideal solution. However, as these new, unplanned settlements arose, the governance of these colonies resulted in dispute. In 1639, a group of representatives from these new settlements near Connecticut convened a meeting to establish a legal code and system of government. The representatives created a document known as the Fundamental Orders of Connecticut, which laid the basis for governing the new settlements. The Fundamental Orders was based on many of the ideas that would later make their way into the Constitution of the United States – ideas such as self-government via elections conducted by secret ballot. Many historians view the Fundamental Orders as the first written constitution in America, and it had the same spirit of independence as the Constitution written 150 years later.

From Colonies to Independence

AD 1773- Boston Tea Party

Shortly after the Fundamental Order of Connecticut was written, the American colonies became a profitable venture for the British Crown. The New World was a source of raw materials, and with settlers arriving daily, the colonies boasted a growing labor pool. These factors led the British government to implement a mercantile economic policy in the colonies. However, many colonists felt that this system overtaxed them without giving them the benefits of being a part of the British Empire. These feelings were particularly strong in Massachusetts, where freedom from royal oversight had always been paramount. A group of Bostonian citizens banded together to alter the opinion of the King, and they took the name "Sons of Liberty". Of particular concern to the colony of Boston was the taxation of essential goods — paper, wax, sugar, and others — but to the colonists, the increased taxation of tea was the most egregious of all. The Sons of Liberty decided to stage a physical protest of the new tax, and on December 16, 1773, a group of these men, disguised as Native Americans, boarded the British cargo ships and dumped the tea chests into Boston Harbor. The protest became known as the Boston Tea Party. This protest set in motion the events that would ultimately lead to the American Revolution.

AD 1774- Coercive Acts empowered by British government

In response to the Boston Tea Party, and in order to reassert control over Boston and persuade other colonies to not follow its rebellious behavior, the British government enacted a series of laws known as the Coercive Acts. These acts were designed to force Boston to submit to the full authority of Britain, and as such, the measures enacted were considerably harsher than any laws that had come before. There were four central provisions in the Coercive Acts, and each had its own intent. The Boston Port Act closed the port of Boston until the tea from the Tea Party had been paid for by the colonists. The Massachusetts Government Act took away the right of the colony to be self-governing. The Administration of Justice Act ensured that British officials in the colonies could not be put on trial for abuses of authority. The Quartering Act allowed for the housing of British soldiers in private homes at the expense of the homeowners. Although these laws, known by the colonists as the Intolerable Acts, were designed to reassert control, they instead spurred the colonists toward greater resistance. Various colonies set up committees of correspondence to enable them to communicate with each other, which eventually led to the creation of the First Continental Congress.

AD 1774- First Continental Congress is convened

From September 5 to October 26, 1774, a group of representatives from various colonies met in Philadelphia, Pennsylvania to address the growing tension between the colonies and Britain. It was hoped that the Congress could negotiate a peaceful settlement with the British that would allow the colonies to continue on as they had in the past — as British citizens but with their daily governance left to themselves. Many believed that the Congress would be able to persuade the British to revoke the Coercive Acts in Massachusetts and that trade relations with Britain could return to normal. However, the Congress was unable to reverse British policy, and so the Congress disbanded, after setting forth an agreement for a meeting of a Second Continental Congress, whose function it would be to oversee continued efforts at peace while simultaneously preparing for what seemed an inevitable conflict with the British.

AD 1775- Battles of Lexington and Concord

While the Second Continental Congress was meeting, the British began taking steps to disarm the local militias of the colonies. The British government feared, as the Congress did, that war was imminent and so they wanted to eliminate the colonies' ability to fight. As such, the British soldiers in Boston, under the command of the military governor General Gage, set out to remove weapons and gunpowder from a militia weapons depot located in the town of Concord. On the evening of April 18, 1775, the British troops moved under the cover of darkness toward the town of Concord. However, thanks to the timely intervention of Paul Revere, a noted Son of Liberty, militias between the Boston coast and Concord were alerted. During the early morning hours of April 19th, militiamen in the town of Lexington blocked the road to Concord. And it was at Lexington that the first shot of the American Revolution was fired. After swiftly dispatching the militia, the British troops marched to Concord, only to find that the weapons had already been moved. During the British march back to Boston, militias attacked the soldiers using hit-and-run tactics, which would be a mainstay of American fighting prowess during the course of the war. Although full-scale war would not yet occur for some time, this battle demonstrated to both sides that the planned-for, but dreaded, war had begun.

AD 1776- Declaration of Independence signed

After the battles of Lexington and Concord, the Second Continental Congress sent a letter to the King known as the "Olive Branch Petition." This petition begged the King to revoke the Coercive Acts in exchange for a colonial resubmission to his authority. However, the Petition fell flat, and the Congress had to take steps to protect the colonies. On July 4, 1776, the Congress adopted the Declaration of Independence, a document which formally severed ties between Britain and the colonies. From the British point of view, this was an act of treason and served only to further their desire to reassert control. For many Americans (as they had begun to think of themselves), this document solidified something they already knew — their subjection to British law was over. As it was considered a document of treason, many members of the Congress were hesitant to sign, until President of the Congress, John Hancock, signed his name in such a large script that his signature would draw the most attention and hopefully, draw most of the king's rage. This move inspired others to sign the document. After the official adoption of the Declaration, copies were quickly delivered to the colonies so that all Americans could be made aware of the events that had transpired. The Declaration of Independence became one of the foundational and pivotal documents of American government.

AD 1777- Articles of Confederation adopted

After the Declaration of Independence was signed but before the war was over, the Second Continental Congress had another major task — to coordinate all thirteen colonies. As the members of the Congress had a great distrust of strong central government, they decided to proceed with a form of governance known as a confederation, a loose grouping of strong states that was overseen, but not controlled by, a central government. The purpose of this central government was to help mediate disputes between colonies, to negotiate with the rest of the world, and to equip, train, and command the army during the war with Britain. The Articles of Confederation put into place a government that, during the war, worked fairly effectively but in the aftermath was too weak to help the newly independent states work cohesively. This weakness led to the creation of the Constitution of the United States.

AD 1781- Battle of Yorktown; British surrender

After six years of desperate struggle and great loss, the American army finally found itself in a strategically superior position to that of the British Army. From September 28 to October 19, 1781, the American army surrounded the city of Yorktown, Virginia, where General Charles Cornwallis and a sizeable contingent of the British army were garrisoned. Thanks in large part to the help of French troops under the command of Jean-Baptiste Donatien de Vimeur, the American army, under the command of George Washington, were able to force Cornwallis to surrender. This surrender led to a cease-fire between armies and was the last major battle of the American Revolution. However, even with the armistice, the war would not officially end until 1783 when the United States signed the Treaty of Paris, formally bringing an end to the conflict and causing Britain to acknowledge America's independence. This treaty allowed the United States to begin the long process of nation building and ensured that America would gain international recognition as a sovereign state.

A Young Nation

AD 1787- Constitutional Convention convened

After the Revolutionary War ended and the United States began learning to live in complete autonomy, the weaknesses of the Articles of Confederation became readily apparent. The Confederation government decided to impanel a group of representatives with the directive of revising the Articles to make them more effective. From May to September 1787, the Constitutional Convention met in Philadelphia, Pennsylvania. Almost from the start, many representatives felt that the Articles were not powerful enough and that the confederate system of government needed to be made over entirely. At the urging of men such as James Madison and Alexander Hamilton, the Convention set out to create an entirely new form of government in great secrecy. At this convention, many pressing issues were set forth and debated, including taxation, slavery, representation in government, and limiting the scope of government. Along with these, parliamentary procedure was formulated in order to most effectively shape the tentative new government into an efficient body. The structure of the government was decided, as well as the division of power within the government. At the end of the Convention, the delegates were sent home in order to get their respective state legislatures to ratify the new Constitution and allow the new government to take effect.

AD 1789- Washington's first term as President begins

After the ratification of the Constitution in 1788, one of the first major tasks for the new government was to elect a president so that the Executive Branch could begin functioning. A tremendously popular war hero and statesman, George Washington won the first American election with one hundred percent of the electoral votes, and he remains the only president ever to do so. Washington was acutely aware of his position in history and his ability to set precedent in regards to the executive. As such, he was diligent in bringing dignity and humility to the office. In light of this position, Washington remains the only president to never be a member of an American political party, as he believed them to be divisive and harmful to the common good. Under Washington's leadership, the First Bank of the United States was chartered. This simple action was highly controversial as this power was not specifically granted to the national government under the terms of the Constitution. In fact, along with the Bill of Rights, no other issue was as formative for American political parties as the Bank of the United States. Ultimately, Washington shaped the presidency into the form it holds today.

AD 1791- First Bank of the United States is created

Perhaps the most controversial move made by George Washington as president was the creation of the First Bank of the United States. The purpose of the Bank, which was chartered in 1791, was to provide an independent entity for the issuance of credit to the American government and foreign nations. This bank would allow the United States to increase the money that it borrowed from investors, both foreign and domestic, meaning that the government would have sufficient funds with which to operate. However, the creation of the Bank was not among the powers given to the government by the Constitution, so there was uncertainty over the legality of this action. On one side stood the Federalists, who supported a broad interpretation of the Constitution, and therefore supported the creation of the Bank, as they believed it was in line with the spirit of the Constitution. On the other side of the issue were the Anti-Federalists, who favored a literal interpretation of the Constitution, and with that, a strictly controlled and limited government. As such, this group stood against the Bank, as they believed it opened a path to an ever-enlarging government. A vitriolic debate took place in the public eye, with men on both sides publishing letters and articles in support of their cause. Eventually, the Federalists won the debate, and the Bank was chartered.

AD 1791- Bill of Rights ratified

Another major event that occurred in 1791 was the ratification of the Bill of Rights, which became the first ten amendments to the Constitution. In 1787, after the Constitutional Convention was recessed, a period of time passed prior to the creation of the United States government as we know it today. In order for the Constitution to take effect, nine of the thirteen states needed to ratify the Constitution. Unfortunately, only five states did so quickly and willingly. The other eight states had hesitations, as they believed the Constitution gave too much power to the national government and did not provide enough protection for the people. In order to address these concerns, a series of amendments, or changes to the Constitution, were drafted. These ten amendments, which became known as the Bill of Rights, specifically prevent the United States government from contravening the rights presented therein. Although these amendments could not be added to the Constitution until the Constitution was ratified, a deal was made wherein the Bill of Rights would be immediately presented upon ratification of the Constitution. As such, four more states ratified the Constitution, and it became the law of the land. As promised, the Bill of Rights was immediately presented to and passed by Congress and then, by Constitutional procedure, was sent to the state legislatures for ratification. Although this process took some time, all thirteen states had ratified the Constitution and the Bill of Rights by 1791.

AD 1796- First political parties appear during a presidential election

George Washington had a remarkable presidency in many ways, not the least of which was the fact that he was a genuinely reluctant to be president. The old maxim, "Power corrupts and absolute power corrupts absolutely," amazingly did not apply to Washington. In fact, Washington did not want to serve a second term but did so at the urging of the country. And so, he served a second term, which lasted until 1796. Washington had never supported the idea of political parties, and as such, he had never joined one. However, many leaders in America at the time felt that political parties allowed them to voice their opinions more strongly and effectively. Two of the most famous men in the government at the time were John Adams, who had been Washington's Vice President and was a Federalist, and Thomas Jefferson, Washington's Secretary of State and an Anti-Federalist (or a Republican as they called themselves). Both men firmly believed in the ascendancy, and correctness, of their political party's belief system. During the election, which ran from November 4th to December 7th, Madison tried to cast Jefferson as anti-government, and Jefferson tried to cast Madison as anti-citizen. This election proved important in the history of America as it set a precedent of the servitude of a candidate to his political party's ideology. The election itself was fairly bitter, and both sides adopted a "must-win" attitude — something that carried over into modern America. The election was unique in that it is the only time that a president and vice president came from different political parties.

AD 1803- *Marbury v. Madison* Supreme Court decision

Despite the fact that the Constitution of the United States calls for the creation and empowerment of a Supreme Court, the Court had played a minor role in the development of the country during the earliest years of its existence. During John Adams' second term as president, he appointed a man named William Marbury as a justice in the courts in Washington, D.C. He assigned his Secretary of State, James Madison, to deliver the official appointment to Marbury, but Madison refused to do so. In response, Marbury sued Madison in the Supreme Court for the right to his commission. Ultimately, the Court decided that Marbury could not legally challenge Madison in the Supreme Court, and so Marbury was not given a legal victory. However, the Court found the law by which Marbury sued Madison to be illegal itself, and as such, the Court struck down the law. This practice became known as judicial review. Although the power of judicial review had not been listed in the Constitution, the Court, as the interpreter of the Constitution, had the ability to issue itself this power, meaning that only by Constitutional Amendment could the ruling be overturned. This case was named *Marbury v. Madison*, and stands as one of the most momentous decisions in the history of the Supreme Court. This precedent of judicial review has become one of the most important functions of the Supreme Court today, as it allows the Court to have oversight of the laws passed by the legislative and executive branches of government.

AD 1812- War of 1812

After the United States had gained its independence from Britain, Europe underwent a great upheaval. First, the French Revolution caused significant harm to political ideologies and to European trade. After the Revolution, first France, and then most of Europe fell under the power of Napoleon Bonaparte. Napoleon instituted a trade embargo known as the Continental System to weaken Britain (which remained free from French control) by cutting off its trade and access to raw materials. As such, the British economy began to suffer greatly. The British government was desperate for a solution to this problem and turned toward the New World for an answer. The British government decided that it needed to subjugate America in order to regain control of its resources. However, Britain did not wish an all-out conflict, as its military had been weakened by the conflict in Europe. The United States misunderstood the intentions of the British and sent Britain a declaration of war. Neither side desired to fight, so much of the War of 1812 was spent in minor skirmishes. But due to poor American naval strategy, the British were able to sail up the Potomac River and burn the White House. For a time, it appeared that America would be defeated, but after the fall of Napoleon in 1814, Britain no longer had a reason to go to war, and they resumed normal trade with the United States, beginning a strategic partnership that still remains in force.

AD 1820- Missouri Compromise enacted

One of the key social and economic issues facing the United States during its formative years was slavery. Although the Constitution allowed slavery and prohibited laws regarding changes in slavery from being made for the first twenty years of Union, the matter of slavery in new states and territories was a pressing one. Both those in favor of slavery and those opposed sought to control the issue as new states were added to the Union. By 1819, there were eleven states that allowed slavery and eleven that did not. Thus, when Missouri applied for statehood with the intention of becoming a slave state, the tension between both sides elevated. Congress battled over this issue until a compromise, thereafter known as the Missouri Compromise, was found. Missouri would be admitted as a slave state, and Maine would be admitted as a free state. In addition, the northern portion of the Louisiana Territory would be free of slavery while the southern portion would support it. This compromise was important because it allowed the United States to maintain peaceful relation between states while both sides of the issue sought alternatives in the long-term.

AD 1854- Kansas-Nebraska Act signed into law

Despite the temporary success of the Missouri Compromise, the issue of slavery became more and more pressing and divided the nation as the United States continued to grow in population as well as wealth. Of particular importance were the territories of Kansas and Nebraska, as both were not yet admitted to the Union and became a battleground for the issue. Rather than simply force a decision upon the territories, Congress believed that giving each territory the right to decide (an idea known as popular sovereignty) would ease tensions in the region. And so, the Kansas-Nebraska Act was passed. This act overturned the Missouri Compromise, by allowing states the right to decide internally. Despite the intentions of Congress, this act caused a great deal of strife and outright violence. The dispute reached such a level of violence that the conflict became known as "Bleeding Kansas" due to the number of casualties caused in skirmishes over the issue of sovereignty. The unwillingness of either side to peacefully reconcile was one of the major factors that led to the Civil War in 1861.

AD 1857- *Dred Scott v. Sandford* Supreme Court Decision

In 1857, a case of monumental importance was brought before the Supreme Court. The case, *Dred Scott v. Sandford*, came about when a slave, Dred Scott, sued the wife of his deceased owner for his freedom. Scott had been taken by his master to a free territory in what one day would become Minnesota. After his master died, Scott sought legal recourse to his freedom. However, when the case reached the Supreme Court, the Court under Chief Justice Roger Taney found that Scott could not sue Sandford, as African Americans were not viewed as citizens and therefore did not have the right to bring legal action in a court of law. This case stands out in American history, as it not only relegated an entire race of people to non-citizen status but also heightened the tension between abolitionists and those who were pro-slavery. Many historians credit the Dred Scott decision as a major precipitating factor of the Civil War.

AD 1861- Civil War begins

In 1860, Abraham Lincoln ascended to the office of president. As a Republican, Lincoln was feared to be an abolitionist by southern, slave-holding states. Before Lincoln could even take office, South Carolina seceded from the Union. Florida, Georgia, Louisiana, Alabama, Texas, and Mississippi followed soon after and declared their secession from the Union. In February of 1861, the Confederacy chose Jefferson Davis as their president. In April of 1861, the Union Fort Sumter in South Carolina requested a resupply-mission by Union forces. The Confederacy saw this attempt as the beginning of war and attacked the fort. When Lincoln sent troops to recapture the fort, other slave-holding states seceded from the Union. From that point until 1865, the United States would find itself embroiled in the bloodiest conflict in its history. The course of the war saw the making of heroes on both sides of the conflict—notably the honorable conduct of Robert E. Lee as the leader of the Virginian army. Villains were also made—notably William Tecumseh Sherman who burned the city of Atlanta to the ground, and the bombing of Richmond by Ulysses Grant. Battles such as Gettysburg and Antietam saw more bloodshed than any American army would ever see again and became rallying cries for both sides. Gettysburg became the site of a national cemetery and Lincoln's famous "Gettysburg Address" while places like Cold Harbor and Cowpens became known for the pointless slaughter that took place there. The Civil War was not only a turning point in American history because it ended the practice of slavery, but because it gave a final answer to the question of state versus national supremacy, with the national government asserting control over the states.

AD 1863- Emancipation Proclamation issued

Although there were other factors that cause the Civil War, none captured the heart of the common citizen like slavery. As the war entered its third year, the Union had become discouraged by the lack of progress in battle and the stubborn refusal of the Confederacy to submit. In order to boost morale and help persuade Delaware, Missouri, Kentucky, and Maryland not to join the rebellion, Lincoln issued the Emancipation Proclamation on January 1, 1863. The Emancipation Proclamation freed all slaves in states that were in rebellion and allowed those freed slaves to join the Union Army as paid soldiers. Although slavery was still allowed in the states that were not rebelling, the Emancipation Proclamation opened the possibility for slaves in those rebel states to escape and become legally free. Although it was an executive order and not a law (as it was not passed by Congress), it effectively reversed the Dred Scott decision by giving slaves their personhood back. The Proclamation was the first step in bringing about civil rights for African Americans, and it was followed by the 13th through 15th Amendments, which codified the citizenship and voting rights of African Americans. Although the Proclamation did not bring an end to the war, it gave the Union a boost and helped the overall course of the war shift in the Union's favor.

AD 1865- Lincoln assassinated and Reconstruction begins

On April 9, 1865 in Appomattox Court House, Virginia, General Robert E. Lee surrendered to Ulysses S. Grant, bringing about an armistice between the Union and the Confederacy. Although a long process remained before the rebelling states rejoined the Union, the surrender was a victory and considered to be the end of the war. Before the war had ended, Lincoln and his advisors sought a plan to reintegrate the Confederate states into the Union swiftly to make the reunion as easy as possible, with the hope of putting behind the hatred that had led to war. This plan was known as "Reconstruction." Many of Lincoln's advisors, as well as members of Congress, felt that the Confederate states needed to be punished and "put in place" as a consequence of the war. As the war ended, the Union began to celebrate victory. As a part of that celebration, Lincoln chose to attend a play "Our American Cousin", at Ford's Theater in Washington, D.C. on April 14th. During the play, a Confederate sympathizer, John Wilkes Booth (who was also an actor), assassinated Lincoln. Booth then leaped to the balcony and shouted, "Sic semper tyrannis" ("Thus always to tyrants"). He jumped onto the stage and made an escape. Eventually, Booth was found and shot. Lincoln died early in the morning on April 15th at the home of William Petersen, which was across the street from Ford's Theater. After Lincoln's death, his Vice President Andrew Johnson assumed the Presidency and took up responsibility for Reconstruction. After much great debate and the passage of many years, Reconstruction ended in 1870, when the last of the Confederate states ratified the 13th through 15th Amendments and were readmitted to the Union.

The Nation Grows

AD 1869- First Transcontinental Railroad completed

One of the keys to the defeat of the Confederacy during the Civil War turned out to be one of the reasons why America became such a powerful, and large, nation. The Union Army was quite adept at building railroads with which they could transport huge numbers of men and large amounts of supplies almost anywhere in the country quickly and easily. Even as the Civil War raged on, the Union was busy constructing the Transcontinental Railroad, which would link the East and West Coast and allow settlement of the American West. As Reconstruction was coming to an end, work on the railroad intensified, and on May 10, 1869 at Promontory Summit in Utah, the eastern and western portions of the railroad finally met. In a large ceremony, a golden spike was driven to complete the final linkage of both arms of the railroad. The completion of the railroad signaled the beginning of intercontinental trade and transport and heralded the beginning of the Gilded Age in America.

AD 1870- Gilded Age begins

With the completion of the Transcontinental Railroad and the end of Reconstruction, America entered a 30-year period called the "Gilded Age." This period lasted from approximately 1870 to 1900. Although this time was marked with many serious social and economic problems, it was also seen as a time of hope, growth, and progress. It is known as the Gilded Age because gilding is the process of covering cheaper metals with a thin layer of gold to mask the flaws of the base metal, and this was true of the time period as well. The problems faced by the nation- workers' rights, Native American Affairs, and settling the west, to name a few, were often masked by the technological progress of the time. The Gilded Age was the age of the robber barons, but it was also the age of Edison and Alexander Graham Bell. At the same time, the income gap between the rich and poor was growing ever wider, but life was simultaneously getting easier for the working class thanks to advances in medicine, food storage, and electricity. Furthermore, this era saw an unprecedented upswing in the number of immigrants, leading to a growth of large cities and a decrease in labor wages. In short, the Gilded Age was a time of vast contradictions, a time of abrupt change, and a time for America to focus inward prior to the external events forced on it by the upcoming century.

AD 1870- Standard Oil Co. created

At the same time that the Transcontinental Railroad was being finished, a new industry was being born in American—the oil industry. In 1870, John D. Rockefeller created the Standard Oil Company. Not only did Standard Oil become the largest refiner in the world, but it also created a new method of doing business called horizontal integration. Horizontal integration occurs when one company buys up all of its competitors, making it a monopoly, thus allowing it to set the market price for its good. In this case, Standard Oil controlled close to ninety percent of the oil in America, meaning that oil prices were set as high as the company chose. This method of doing business made Rockefeller the richest man in America, and many speculate, the richest man in history. However, Rockefeller and other men like him became known for harsh, questionable, and often illegal business practices, and thus this group of elite business owners became known as the robber barons-a reference to their wealth being derived from the "theft" from others. In 1911, the Standard Oil Corporation was broken up when the Supreme Court ruled that its business practices made it a monopoly and therefore were illegal. Standard Oil serves as a prime example of the disconnect between business owners and their workers, and these differences led to great tension in the United States during the Gilded Age.

AD 1875- Carnegie opens first steel mill

Another businessman who shaped the face of modern America was Andrew Carnegie, a Scottish immigrant. Where Rockefeller was interested in oil, Carnegie was interested in another emerging good — steel. Carnegie was an astute businessman who knew that steel would become the lifeblood of the rail industry and therefore become the backbone of transportation across the United States. Where Rockefeller bought out his competitors, Carnegie focused on a strategy of vertical integration or the buying up of all of the industries needed to support his industry. And so, Carnegie bought railroads, coal mines, and steel mills in support of his expansion program. In 1875, Carnegie opened his first steel mill and revolutionized not only the steel industry but industry in general. Carnegie was obsessed with efficiency and maximizing work (and therefore profit). He realized that it was more cost effective to run his factory continuously all day every day, as the extra work would more than make up for the extra cost of replacing his machines more frequently. However, he treated his workers in a similar fashion. Workers who were not totally efficient and focused despite the horribly inhospitable working conditions were summarily dismissed. Those injured on the job were also dismissed, as there was no protection for them in place at the time. In fact, Carnegie's treatment of his workers went a long way, pushing workers to organize into labor unions, and these unions would help shape the landscape of industrial America into modern times.

AD 1876- Telephone invented

Of all of the inventions of the 19th century, perhaps none has such importance or lasting effect as the telephone. As rail lines began to crisscross America and the telegraph became a ubiquitous part of the American experience, new and faster forms of communications were sought. Although many attempts were made at transporting the human voice electrically across long distances, it was Alexander Graham Bell who first patented an electrical telephone in 1876. His first fully successful test of the device made famous the phrase, "Watson, come here! I want to see you!" From that time forward, the telephone revolutionized communication and the American way of life. Suddenly, the vast distances between cities in America were no longer a hindrance, and people could share experiences even without physical proximity. The improved speed of communication also allowed governments to be more responsive to its constituents and for those constituents to be able to more fully vocalize their needs. Finally, as information and communication is essential for a military force, this advance helped propel the American military to preeminence among world powers.

AD 1892- Homestead Strike

As Carnegie revolutionized the steel industry with more and more advanced technology, he required less and less skilled workers to operate his factories. As such, he was less willing to pay skilled ironworkers and brought in unskilled labor to man the machines. Unsurprisingly, the ironworkers union was furious at this treatment, and the workers at Carnegie's Homestead steel plant organized a strike. The strike lasted from June 30 to July 6, 1892. On July 6th, a battle broke out between the union workers and a security force known as the Pinkertons (from the Pinkerton National Detective Agency). Over the course of the day, several gunfights broke out. The Pinkertons eventually surrendered, forcing Governor Pattison to bring in the state militia, which cause an end to the strike. A total of sixteen men were killed. The Homestead Strike and resulting battle led to a weakening of the steel union, which had a trickle-on effect with many other unions in America of weakening the position of workers who wished to bargain collectively for better treatment in their respective industries.

AD 1898- Spanish American War

Throughout the Gilded Age, America began to espouse a philosophy called the Monroe Doctrine, named for President James Monroe who first codified the idea. In short, the Monroe Doctrine was based on the premise of hemispheric hegemony, which is the idea that major nations have the right to oversee events in their sphere of influence, while outside nations must keep their distance. Throughout the 1890's, Spain had violated this principal in their treatment of Cuba, which, at the time, was a territorial possession. At the request of Cuba, the United States began sending aid to them. When the American ship the *USS Maine* exploded while at anchor, the United States declared war on Spain. The major thrust of the war was in Cuba itself, where the United States sent the bulk of its troops. During the war, future President Theodore Roosevelt made a name for himself and his personal unit, the Rough Riders. Roosevelt's popularity during the war went a long way in helping him secure the presidency in 1901. The Spanish, outmanned and outgunned, eventually agreed to a ceasefire, and during the treaty phase of negotiations, gave up both Cuba and the Philippines to the United States. The Spanish-American War was the first time that America had demonstrated its modern military prowess and established itself as a world power.

AD 1908- Ford Model T first sold

Henry Ford was an American whose vision of industry transformed the United States for both workers and consumers. Ford, as an automobile manufacturer, knew that if he could reduce the price of his vehicles, he would vastly increase his sales base. He had a vision of America in which every family owned a Ford vehicle. In 1908, Ford introduced the Model T Ford. Although this vehicle was not luxurious, it was simple, easy to operate, and affordable. The vehicle was so popular that Ford had to revolutionize the factory system by introducing the automated production line. Instead of a worker moving from vehicle to vehicle to perform his task, the vehicle would be brought to him, which resulted in much higher efficiency in his workers and a much higher volume of automobiles being produced. The Model T was so successful that between 1908 and 1927 when production ended, over fifteen million Model T's were produced. Because of the success, Ford also revolutionized working conditions in his factory. Workers were paid far more than those in other automobile companies and were even given sick leave-a thing unheard of until that time. When the Great Depression struck, Ford workers were given a raise at a time when almost twenty-five percent of the workforce was unemployed. Many of Ford's innovations, both industrial and employee, shaped America into the workforce that is recognizable today.

AD 1917- American enters World War I

From 1914 until 1918, the world was engaged in the second largest conflict in history — World War I. While primarily a European conflict, battles were also fought in Africa and Asia. Although the conflict centered on the French and British fighting against Germany in the heartland of France, most of the nations in Europe were dragged into the war due to an unwieldy alliance system. The United States, owing to its distance from the conflict, was able to remain neutral for much of the war. However, after the sinking of several ships with American citizens on board, the American attitude began to slowly swing in favor of war. After the United States became aware of a German-sponsored potential invasion of Texas by Mexico, the United States entered the war in 1917. Although American soldiers lacked the experience of their European counterparts, their energy and enthusiasm brought a boost to their allies. But more importantly, the United States brought its formidable manufacturing capability to bear, and the supply of material and arms to its soldiers allowed the American military to make a far greater impact than their small numbers suggested. Following the armistice at 11:11 AM on November 11, 1918, America and its allies met to determine the fate of Germany. America advocated a strategy of rebuilding Germany as an ally to remove the possibility of future conflict. However, the French called strongly for the punishment of Germany for its role in the war. Internal politics prevented America from voicing a stronger opinion, and the treatment of Germany was much what France had demanded — a move that ultimately resulted in World War II.

AD 1920- Roaring Twenties begin

After World War I drew to close, American servicemen returned home, and life went back to normal. However, the war had empowered several minorities, including women and African Americans. After a short recession, America entered a time of economic prosperity, which, coupled with the manufacturing might of the country, led to an unbridled period of consumerism. This consumerism, along with the social movements of the time led to the era being known as the "Roaring Twenties." During this period, several important social movements took place. For women, the flappers represented an end to the repressive social mores of traditional American culture and gave women a voice louder than they had ever previously had. The movement eventually led to the passage of the 19th Amendment, which gave women in America the right to vote for the first time in its history. For African Americans, the Harlem Renaissance was an artistic movement that gave African Americans a strong voice in shaping American culture. The Roaring Twenties were also a time of much illicit activity, as Prohibition forced people who imbibed alcohol to do so secretly, often at clubs called speakeasies. Despite the veneer of beauty and excitement of the Roaring Twenties, the flashiness of the era in truth hid many severe problems that the nation would be confronted with during the Great Depression of the 1930's.

AD 1929- Stock Market Crash and beginning of Great Depression

During the 1920's, many businesses and banks began engaging in very risky investment behaviors in order to encourage consumerism. Extending credit to those who could not afford the terms was common, and investing in the stock market using credit became a regular occurrence. Due to the inflation caused by the over-extension of credit, and the cyclical slowing of the economy, the Roaring Twenties came to a drastic halt on October 24, 1929. On this date, the stock market crashed, and much of the value in the American economy evaporated literally overnight. And, with banks unable to meet the demand for cash withdrawals, a time known as the Great Depression began. The Great Depression was made worse by a concurrent drought throughout the American Midwest and West that was was so terrible it became known as the "Dust Bowl." During this time, as many as twenty-five percent of the American workforce was laid-off since businesses no longer had enough customers to maintain their employees in paid positions. And so, the early 1930's was a time of deep economic despair, starvation, and hopelessness. And, until the intervention of America's new president, Franklin Delano Roosevelt (also called FDR), the plight of America seemed unsolvable.

AD 1933- New Deal begins

On March 4, 1933, Franklin Delano Roosevelt took his oath of office and became President of the United States. Immediately, FDR undertook a series of measures and reforms that we designed to bring America out of the Great Depression and prevent another depression from ever occurring again. This program was known as the New Deal, because it was a "new deal" between the American government and the American people. The New Deal provided work for those who could not otherwise find employment and had these workers engaged in infrastructure projects to fully modernize and beatify America. While some people built roads and bridges, others planted forests and maintained national parks. Still others were tasked with improving schools and hospitals within their own communities. Beyond simply providing work, the New Deal sought to protect the most vulnerable members of society. Social Security, which is retirement insurance, was created, as well as protections for banks to ensure that Americans would always have access to their hard-earned money. Although many found the New Deal to be a great overreach by the federal government and questioned its efficacy, what cannot be denied is that the New Deal allowed America to put itself in a position to exploit the financial opportunity of World War II.

America as a World Leader

AD 1941- Japanese attack on Pearl Harbor

On September 1, 1939, World War II began when Germany invaded Poland. Just as it had during the outbreak of World War I, the United States managed to keep itself out of the conflict with the war taking place in Europe, Africa, and Asia. However, due to American economic embargo of Japan, the Japanese seeking conquest in the Pacific, were forced to attack America in the hope that it would end the embargo and allow them to gather the resources necessary for conquest. On December 7, 1941 at 7:48 AM, Japanese bombers attacked the American naval base at Pearl Harbor, Hawaii. During the attack, eight battleships and three cruisers were sunk and further 188 aircraft were destroyed. This attack led to the American entrance into World War II on December 8th when Congress declared war on both Japan and Germany. Harnessing the incredible manufacturing power that America had built during the Great Depression, America systematically set out to out-build and overpower its enemies. During the course of the war, America demonstrated that modern warfare was about three basic things: amount of materiel (arms and other weapons) available, the communication between commanders and soldiers, and the speed of an army's advance. These ideas dispelled the historical view of warfare that said that advanced technology and highly soldiers always won a war. And so, despite Germany's technological advantage and superior training, the United States defeated it.

AD 1945- America uses first atomic weapons

After the defeat of Germany in World War II, American turned its full attention toward defeating Japan. Given the religious and militaristic Japanese culture, America struggled to dislodge Japan from its many occupied territorial possessions. However, with sheer willpower, America pushed Japan back onto its home islands, at which point America had to contemplate an invasion of Japan itself. American strategists estimated that an invasion of Japan might cost as many as a million American lives. With this possibility, President Truman sought an alternative. Throughout the course of the war, America had been working on a secret super weapon, the atomic bomb. This weapon was designed to destroy an entire city with one bomb and cause such fear that an enemy would immediately surrender upon its threat of use. In order to demonstrate the effectiveness of this weapon to Japan, American dropped an atomic bomb on the Japanese city of Hiroshima on Aug 6, 1945, at 8:15 AM and the city was instantly destroyed. There were approximately 146,000 casualties as a result of this one bomb. America then sent an ultimatum to Japan that anything short of unconditional surrender would result in another bombing. When Japan failed to surrender, America dropped a second weapon. On August 9th at 11:02 AM, this second weapon destroyed the Japanese city of Nagasaki, with a total of approximately 80,000 casualties. After this, Japan surrendered, and World War II came to an end. The beginning of the nuclear age was a significant factor in the eventual Cold War, which would shape world events for around the next fifty years.

AD 1947- Truman Doctrine and Marshall Plan outline foreign policy

After the United States ended World War II with the dropping of the atomic bombs, an era known as the Cold War began. This was not a direct conflict, but rather an ideological competition between the forces of communism and the forces of capitalism. As neither side could launch an attack without the assurance of being destroyed by the other side's weapons, a stalemate occurred. Instead of fighting, both sides sought to create more allies and to have their ideas outgrow the other side's, to isolate and ultimately bringing them to an end. The United States, as the center of capitalist ideology, attempted to sway nations that were well within the Soviet (communist) sphere of influence. On March 12, 1947, President Truman addressed a full session of Congress to propose aid to the nations of Turkey and Greece, which had been ravaged by World War II and were being threatened by a possible communist takeover. This address became known as the Truman Doctrine and said that America would give both military and economic aid to any country that desired to remain free from communism. A year later, Secretary of State George Marshall gave a commencement address at Harvard University in which he laid out a plan for rebuilding any nation affected by World War II, including the Soviet Union if it had asked (which it never did). This plan for aid, called the Marshall Plan, was also a plan of action to make allies, which would eliminate the possibility of another world war, and help isolate the Soviet Union and its communist ideals. The Truman Doctrine and the Marshall Plan formed the basis for American foreign policy for well over forty years.

AD 1955- Rosa Parks and the bus boycott

At the same time, America was helping its allies rebuild after World War II, it was lagging far behind in social equality. Despite the contributions of African Americans to World War II and the Korean War, the racial gap in America had widened during the 1950's to the point that African Americans were not allowed to use the same drinking fountains, attend the same schools, or sit in preferential seats on public transportation. And so, in 1955, an event occurred that would lead to the Civil Rights Movement and eventually bring racial equality. On December 1st in the city of Birmingham, Alabama, an African America seamstress named Rosa Parks boarded a bus to go home from work. Because she was tired, she refused to vacate the seat for a white passenger. Eventually, the police were called and Parks was arrested for the crime of sitting wrongfully on a bus. Because Parks had been an active member of a civil rights group, she was aware of the precedent she was setting, which stiffened her resolve. Due to Parks' arrest, the Civil Rights Movement in Birmingham instituted an African-American boycott of the bus service until such time as the bus laws were repealed. In 1956, the Supreme Court found the Birmingham laws to be illegal, and they were overturned. This led to great tension between African Americans and whites in the South and was a precipitating factor in the Civil Rights Movement. Rosa Parks' conduct was an inspiration for Martin Luther King, Jr., who would go on to be the public face of the movement in the 1960's.

AD 1968- Martin Luther King, Jr. assassinated

The 1960's were a challenging time for the United States. Embroiled in the Vietnam War, the Space Race, and the Cold War, the United States was also reeling from social unrest. The Civil Rights Movement, which had begun the 1950's had reached full swing, and there were riots, protests, and violence in the streets in many Southern states. Although many civil rights leaders advocated peaceful resistance (most notably Martin Luther King, Jr.), the idea of civil rights and equal integration into society was anathema to many Southern whites. On April 4, 1968, King was assassinated at his motel in Memphis, Tennessee by an escaped convict named James Earl Ray. King's death was a setback for the Civil Rights Movement as it created a vacuum in the power structure of the movement, one that was filled by leaders with much more extreme and violent methods of securing civil rights. The elevation of these leaders meant that the Civil Rights Movement of the 1970's would be significantly more violent and focused on revenge rather than growth. However, King's death was not simply a loss for the Civil Rights Movement, but for America as a whole because he had been a remarkable leader and statesman, who likely would have persuaded Congress to pass equal rights legislation—something that was set back years due to his untimely death.

AD 1969- Moon landing

July 20, 1969 marked a first in human history. For the very first time, a human set foot on another world. In the 1960's there had been a competition known as the Space Race between America and Russia as part of the Cold War. The objective was to be the first country to land on the moon. Both countries spent the decade and billions of dollars creating spacecraft capable of reaching, and landing on the moon. However, the free market system of American capitalism provided faster and larger technical leaps than the Soviets could manage, thus allowing Americans to reach the moon first. On July 20th, Neil Armstrong became the first man to walk on the moon, and his first words, "That's one small step for [a] man, one giant leap for mankind," became immortalized. His companion Edwin "Buzz" Aldrin became the second man to walk on the moon. Both men stayed on the surface for just over two hours, collected several rock samples, and planted an American flag. Afterward, they returned to their craft, and several days later, returned to earth. During the landing and spacewalk, the whole world joined together to celebrate this momentous occasion, and few events in history have had a similar effect. Armstrong and Aldrin paved the way for further exploration of the moon, and eventually, other parts of the solar system. The impact of the moon landing can still be felt today, as America again prepares to start sending humans to the moon.

AD 1975- Vietnam War ends

After World War II and the swiftly following Korean War, America entered a time of relative peace. However, starting in 1955, a conflict in Vietnam would eventually drag America into war once again. Throughout the 1960's and early 1970's, America had a large military presence in Vietnam as a result of the Truman Doctrine. The Vietnam War, which ran from 1955 to 1975, was a conflict between the forces of capitalism and those of communism and was part of the overall Cold War pattern of indirect confrontation. This war fundamentally changed the relationship between American citizens and their government, as the citizenry vocally and violently did not support the conflict while the American government supported it passionately. The draft was still in force during most of the conflict, meaning that young men could be made to go to war, regardless of their opinions about the matter. Because the war was a guerilla war, the tactics used were often grotesque and seen as immoral. As more and more soldiers were killed in the fight to control the jungle (where most of the conflict took place), the American people became angrier and angrier with the American government for being unresponsive to the will of the people. This distrust of government shaped the attitudes of many Americans in the 1970's and 1980's, and this was felt particularly strongly in music, where the theme of rebellion was championed. In 1975, the communist forces of North Vietnam overran the capitalistic South Vietnam, unifying the country under the banner of communism. This was perhaps the most difficult defeat in war for America since early battles of the American Revolution.

AD 1981- Reagan becomes president

The mid to late 1970's were a time of relative peace and stability between America and the Soviet Union, and this period was known as détente. America and Russia had conducted a joint mission in space and were working on trade agreements and nuclear weapons disarmament talks. In 1981, a former governor from California, Ronald Reagan was elected president. Reagan believed fundamentally that, the Soviet Union was the "Evil Empire" — as he labeled it during a speech — and that both ideologies could not coexist. As such, Reagan began a program to bring the Soviet Union to its knees. Reagan called for the construction of a 600-ship navy and began developing a series of new, highly sophisticated weapons with which to attack the Soviet Union. Reagan also proposed a new technology called the Strategic Defensive Initiative (also called Star Wars), which would position a series of lasers in space in orbit around earth. This shield of lasers was designed to shoot down any Russian atomic missiles, theoretically providing America a means to "win" a nuclear war. Russia, in response to Reagan, began a massive buildup of its own, and relations between the two nations became decidedly hostile. What America did not know was that Russia bankrupted itself during this arms race and did not pose a fraction of the threat envisioned by Reagan. However, this financial hardship would force Russia to change its outlook, and eventually collapse in 1991 (after Reagan's retirement), bringing an end to the Cold War.

AD 1991- First Gulf War in Iraq

Throughout the Cold War, the United States provided weapons to any country that claimed friendship and a willingness to reject communism. As a result, many nations that might otherwise have hated America were coopted as allies. However, when the Cold War ended and the threat of nuclear annihilation passed, many of those nations turned against the United States. One of these countries was Iraq. Throughout the 1970's and 1980's, America supported Iraq against its neighbor Iran, which was decidedly pro-communism at that point. However, after the Iran-Iraq War, Saddam Hussein, the leader of Iraq, turned his attention toward a weak but wealthy neighbor, Kuwait. In 1990, Iraq invaded Kuwait for its expansive oil fields. The United States, in order to protect its ally Kuwait, the stability of the region, and the flow of oil set out to retake Kuwait from Iraq. This action, which took place in late 1990, was known as Desert Shield — a nod towards the idea of protecting the innocent Kuwaiti people. After swiftly retaking Kuwait, the United States turned its attention toward forcing Iraq to surrender, and in early 1991, began Operation Desert Storm, which was meant to capture the Iraqi capital of Baghdad. In one of the quickest wars in history, America crushed the Iraqi army and forced Hussein to surrender. After this, America set up peace-keeping operations in the region, and, until 2003, a time of relative stability existed in the region.

AD 2001- 9/11 Terrorist Attacks

On September 11, 2001, a group from the terrorist organization al-Qaeda hijacked four American aircraft. Two of these planes destroyed the World Trade Center Twin Towers while another hit the Pentagon. The fourth plane, believed to be headed towards the White House, was recaptured by passengers and crashed into a field in Pennsylvania. During these attacks, 2,977 people were killed. Thereafter, the United States launched a "War on Terror," which started in Afghanistan and spread to Iraq. Over the course of the next decade, the United States would continue to seek out terrorists and bring them to justice. On December 3, 2003, Saddam Hussein was captured. On December 30th, he was executed for crimes against humanity by the Iraqi people. On May 2, 2011, Osama bin Laden, the al-Qaeda leader responsible for the 9/11 attacks, was located and killed by United States Special Forces Seal Team Six. Along with various other terrorist leaders that had been captured or killed, al-Qaeda lost its power, but in its wake, organizations like ISIL (also called ISIS) found a following and started gaining influence. Although the war on terror is officially over, the United States maintains vigilance in the hopes of never repeating an experience like 9/11.

AD 2007- The Great Recession begins

Despite the War on Terror, the late 1990's and early 2000's marked a period of economic growth for the United States. During this time, investor confidence was high, and lending institutions, falsely believing that the economic growth would continue unchecked, began a series of highly risky lending practices, including giving out mortgage loans that far exceeded the recipient's ability to repay. Beyond that, many investors began taking on assets that were toxic (i.e. they no longer held value due to changes in the market). As a result of these actions, the United States saw a huge drop in the housing market in mid-2007, coupled with a huge drop in the financial market. Overnight, many investors lost between 30 and 90 percent of their investments. Not since the Great Depression had the American economy taken such a drastic loss, which is why that time is referred to as the "Great Recession". Because of lessons learned during the Great Depression, the American government began buying up bad loans, mortgages, and investments, spending 800 billion dollars to prevent the entire American economy from collapsing. Although not quite as severe as the Great Depression, the Great Recession saw the highest level of unemployment since the 1940's. As many as ten percent of the American workforce went unemployed, and the stock market tumbled. If not for the recovery efforts of the American government with programs such as TARP, it is likely that the United States economy would have fully collapsed. Even with these vast efforts by the government, the United States is still feeling the effects of the Great Recession, and unemployment continues to be a serious problem.

AD 2008- Barack Obama elected president

In 2008, history was made when Barack Obama was the first African-American to be elected president. Running on an almost-populist or progressive platform, Obama sought the votes of the disenfranchised (both economically and socially) and was able to woo minorities. After defeating Hillary Clinton in the Democratic Primary Election, Obama ran against Senator McCain and Alaska governor Sarah Palin. Thanks to a brilliant use of social media, coupled with a message of change ("Yes we can"), Obama won by the largest margin a Democrat had enjoyed since Lyndon Johnson in the 1960's. Obama's election was a victory for civil rights and went a long way in closing the racial gap that still exists in the United States. Obama inherited the Great Recession, and despite having a Republican Congress, helped the United States regain much of its lost economy. As he remains the sitting president, it will be for future generations to fully see the impact of his presidency, but, it must be said, he has faced great challenges as president and has helped shape America for years to come.

Made in the USA
Lexington, KY
20 January 2017